ETERNAL SECURITY

ETERNAL SECURITY

H. A. Ironside

LOIZEAUX BROTHERS
Neptune, New Jersey

First Edition, July 1934
Revised Edition, May 1986

LOIZEAUX BROTHERS, Inc.
*A Nonprofit Organization Devoted to the Lord's Work,
and to the Spread of His Truth*

Library of Congress Cataloging-in-Publication Data

Ironside, H. A. (Henry Allan), 1876-1951.
   Eternal security.

   Rev. ed. of: The eternal security of the believer.
   1. Assurance (Theology)   2. Predestination.
I. Ironside, H. A. (Henry Allan), 1876-1951.
Eternal security of the believer.   II. Title.
BT785.I695   1986   234   86-2757
ISBN 0-87213-347-8 (pbk.)

97 96 95 94 93 92 91

12 11 10 9 8 7 6 5 4 3

PRINTED IN THE UNITED STATES OF AMERICA

FOREWORD

This pamphlet consists of an address delivered in the D. L. Moody Memorial Church on a Lord's Day morning and the substance of two Bible hours at the Friday lecture meeting when questions were submitted and were answered from the platform. Careful editing might properly have eliminated everything that looks like repetition. But inasmuch as it is by constant re-affirmation that truth finds lodgment in the mind and heart, I have not pruned the answers as much as I otherwise might have done. Let me say that my object was not controversy nor the besting of an opponent but rather the edification and enlightenment of the people of God, that the knowledge of the truth might deliver from legality and give true liberty.

H. A. IRONSIDE

Chicago, Illinois, April 24, 1934.

ETERNAL SECURITY

An Address by Dr. H. A. Ironside in the
D. L. Moody Memorial Church

Can a Believer Ever Be Lost?

It has been announced that I will speak to you on a subject which has occasioned a good deal of controversy among the people of God. I want to take as a starting point—not exactly as a text, because we shall be looking at a good many Scriptures—Romans 8:38-39: "For I am persuaded, that neither death, nor life, nor angels, nor principalities, nor powers, nor things present, nor things to come, nor height, nor depth, nor any other creature, shall be able to separate us from the love of God, which is in Christ Jesus our Lord." This is the inspired answer to the question of verse 35: "Who shall separate us from the love of Christ?" That is, once we are Christians, once we know the love of Christ, once we have been justified by faith, who is there, what power is there, that can separate from the love of Christ? And the answer, how full, how clear, not a shadow, not a doubt, not a question left, when the apostle says that neither death nor life shall separate! Can you think of anything which is neither included in death nor in life? Neither death nor life shall separate!

No unseen powers can separate the believer from Christ, "neither angels, nor principalities, nor powers." These terms are used again and again in the New Testament, particularly in the Epistles, for angelic hosts, good and evil. When our Savior rose from the dead He spoiled principalities and powers, that is, He defeated all the hosts of evil led by Satan; and so we may take it that the angels referred to here are good angels, and the principalities and powers are possibly evil angels. But there is nothing that good angels would do and nothing that evil angels can do which will result in the separation of the believer from Christ. And then further he says, "neither things present nor things to come." Again let me put the question, Can you think of any experience through which a believer might ever go which is neither a thing present nor a thing to come? And the Holy Ghost says that neither things present nor things to come shall be able to separate us from the love of Christ. As though that were not enough, He speaks in a more general way when He says that neither "height nor depth (nothing in heaven, nothing in hell), nor any other created thing, shall be able to separate us from the love of God, which is in Christ Jesus our Lord." It looks to me as though we are safe if we are believers in the Lord Jesus Christ.

ETERNAL SECURITY: ITS MEANING

When we speak of the eternal security of the believer, what do we mean? We mean that once a poor sinner has been regenerated by the Word and the Spirit of God, once he has received a new life and a new nature and has been made partaker of the divine nature, once he has been justified from every charge before the throne of God, it is absolutely impossible that that man should ever again be a lost soul. Having said that, let me say what we do not mean when we speak of the eternal security of the believer. We do not mean that it necessarily follows that if one professes to be saved, if he comes out to the front in a meeting, shakes the preacher's hand, and says he accepts the Lord Jesus Christ as his Savior, that that person is eternally safe. It does not mean that if one joins a church or makes a profession of faith, is baptized, becomes a communicant, and takes an interest in Christian work, that that person is forever secure. It does not mean that because one manifests certain gifts and exercises these gifts in Christian testimony, that that person is necessarily eternally secure.

Our Lord Jesus Christ said to the people of His day, as recorded in Matthew 7:21-23: "Not every one that saith unto Me, Lord, Lord, shall enter into the kingdom of heaven; but he that doeth the will of My Father which is in heaven. Many will say to Me in that day, Lord, Lord, have we not prophesied in Thy name? and in Thy name have cast out devils? and in Thy name done many wonderful works? And then will I profess unto them, I never knew you: depart from Me, ye that work iniquity." Such people then may have been very active in what is called Christian work—they have preached, they have cast out demons, that is, their influence has been such that men and women have found deliverance from satanic power through their ministrations in the name of Jesus, they have professed with their lips, they have accomplished many wonderful works, but they are found in that day among the lost, and when they plead their great activity and their earnestness in Christian testimony, the Lord says to them, "I never knew you." Notice, He does not say to them, "I used to know you, but you have forfeited My favor and I do not know you any longer." He says, "I *never* knew you."

THE SHEEP OF CHRIST

You remember how He speaks of His own in John 10:27-30: "My sheep hear My voice, and I know them, and they follow Me: and I give unto them eternal life; and they shall never perish, neither shall any man pluck them out of My hand. My Father, which gave them Me, is greater than all; and no man is able to pluck them out of My Father's hand. I and My Father are one." Of His own He says, "I know them." Of these others, in spite of all their activity, in spite of all their accomplishments, He says in the day of judgment, "I never knew you." That is a very solemn thing. That answers a question that is frequently put to us. I do not know how many times I have had individuals come to me with a hypothetical case like this: "Suppose a man who joined the church, who professed to be saved, who for a number of years was a very active Christian worker, perhaps a Sunday school teacher, perhaps an elder or a deacon in the church, maybe a minister, but after some years of apparent consistent Christian living and helpfulness in testimony he turns his back on it all, returns to the world, utterly repudiates Christianity, and now denies *in toto* the gospel he once professed. How does that square with your doctrine of the eternal security of the believer?" That does not touch the matter at all. The apostle John tells us how we are to understand a case like that. He says in 1 John 2:19, "They went out from us, but they were not of us; for if they had been of us, they would no doubt have continued with us: but they went out, that they might be made manifest that they were not all of us," or literally, "that they were not altogether of us." That is, it is possible to do all the things that I have spoken of and yet never be regenerated. It is quite possible to join a church, to make a Christian profession; it is quite possible to observe the Christian ordinances, to teach and to preach, and yet never be born again. If one teaches and preaches the truth, it will produce good results and will do men good whether the teacher or the preacher be real or not, for it is the truth that God uses. Of course He can use the truth to better advantage when it is proclaimed by a holy man living to the glory of God than when it is proclaimed by a hypocrite. Nevertheless, God uses His truth regardless of who may proclaim it, and that explains how people may do mighty works in the name of Christ and yet never be born again.

CHRIST'S ONE OFFERING

When we say that the believer in the Lord Jesus is eternally secure, we base it upon a number of lines of scriptural testimony. In the first place, we rest it upon the perfection of Christ's one offering upon the cross. Personally, I never can understand how thoughtful people, taught by the Holy Spirit of God, can carefully read the Epistle to the Hebrews and not see that throughout that Epistle the writer is contrasting the many sacrifices offered under law with the one sacrifice of our Lord Jesus Christ. That to which he particularly calls attention is this: under law every time an Israelite sinned, he needed a new sin offering, and every year the nation had to celebrate the great day of atonement when a new offering was presented to God for the people. Why? Because those sacrifices could never take away sin, they simply covered sin for the time being. But we are told in Hebrews 10 that when the Lord Jesus Christ came into the world and offered Himself without spot to God, the effect of His sacrifice was eternal. Verse 14 makes this clear: "For by one offering He hath perfected for ever them that are sanctified." Perfected for how long? "Oh," says somebody, "as long as they are faithful." No, that is not what it says. "He hath perfected for ever." Why? Because the sacrifice is all-efficacious.

I am sure my brethren who deny the doctrine of the eternal security of the believer do not realize that in so doing they are putting a slight upon the finished work of Christ, they are reducing the sacrifice of Christ practically to the level of the offerings of bulls and goats in the Old Testament dispensation. I am sure they do not mean to do that, for they love their Lord just as truly as I trust I love Him, and they do not want to dishonor Him. But they are afraid that this doctrine will lead people to be careless about their lives, and therefore they stress the possibility of a man losing his salvation after he has once been justified by faith. But they do not pursue that to its logical conclusion; they do not see that it is a practical denial of the finished work of our Lord Jesus Christ. We are saved eternally because the sacrifice of Christ abides.

When I came to the Lord Jesus Christ and put my trust in Him, not only were all my sins up to the day of my conversion forgiven, but all my sins were put away for eternity. When a young Christian, I was taught something like this: I thought when I was converted that all my sins, from the time of dawning accountability up to that night when I put my trust in the Lord Jesus, were put away, and now God had given me a new start, and if I could only keep the record clean to the end of my life, I would get to heaven; but if I did not keep it clean, I ceased to be a Christian and I had to get converted all over again. Every time this happened the past was under the blood, but I had to keep the record clean for the future. What a God-dishonoring view of the atonement of Christ that is! If only those of my sins that were committed up to the moment of my conversion were put away by the atoning blood of Jesus, what possible way would there be by which sins I have confessed after that could be dealt with? The only ground on which God could forgive sin is that Jesus settled all upon the cross, and when I trust Him, all that He has done goes down to my account.

What of Future Sins?

A lady came to me one day and said, "I do not understand you there. I can understand that Christ died for the sins I committed up to the night of my conversion, but do you mean to tell me that Christ died for my future sins?"

I said, "How many of your sins were in the past when Christ died on the cross?"

She looked puzzled for a moment, and then the light broke in, and she said, "How foolish I have been! Of course they were all future when Jesus died for me. I had not committed any of them."

God saw all your sins, and He laid upon Jesus all your iniquity. Therefore, when you trusted Him, you were justified freely from all things. Do you say, "Does it make no difference then if a believer sins?" That is another question, and it would take a whole evening to go into that, but here is the point: the moment you trust the Lord Jesus as your Savior, your responsibility as a sinner having to do with the God of judgment is ended for eternity, but that same moment your responsibility as a child having to do with a Father in heaven begins. Now if as a child you should sin against your Father, God will have to deal with you about that, but as a father and not as a judge. That is a line of truth that stands by itself and does not contradict what I am now teaching. It explains some things that bewilder people when this doctrine is brought before them.

The Spirit's Perseverance

In the second place, we base the doctrine of the eternal security of the believer upon the perseverance and omnipotent power of the Holy Spirit of God. Look at Philippians 1:6. Writing to these saints, the apostle says, when he thanks them for their fellowship in the gospel from the first day until now, "Being confident of this very thing, that He which hath begun a good work in you will perform it until the day of Jesus Christ." Do you see that? Who began the good work in you if you are a believer in the Lord Jesus? The Holy Spirit of God did. It was He who convicted you of sin; it was He who led you to put your trust in Christ; it was He who through the Word gave you the witness that you were saved; it is He who has been conforming you to Christ since you first trusted the Lord Jesus. Having thus taken you up in grace, the Holy Spirit has a definite purpose in view. He is eventually going to conform you fully to the image of the Lord Jesus Christ, and He never begins a work that He does not intend to finish. "Being confident of this very thing, that He which hath begun a good work in you will perform it until the day of Jesus Christ." If when you were a poor sinner the Holy Spirit had power sufficient to break down your opposition to God and to bring to an end your unbelief and rebellion, do you think for one moment that He does not have power enough to subdue your will as a believer and to carry on to completion the work that He began?

People say, "I see you believe in that old Baptist doctrine of 'once in grace, always in grace.'" Or another says, "I understand you hold that old Presbyterian idea of 'the final perseverance of the saints.'" I do not know why this should be called either Baptist or Presbyterian, only to the extent that Baptists and Presbyterians agree with the Book, and the Word of God clearly shows that once God takes us up in grace nothing can separate us from the love of Christ, so that evidently the expression, "once in grace, always in grace," is a perfectly correct one. But, on the other hand, I am not so enthusiastic about the other expression, "the perseverance of the saints." I believe in it; I believe that all saints—all really belonging to God—will persevere to the end, for the Book tells me, "He that shall endure unto the end, the same shall be saved" (Matthew 24:13), and if a man starts out and makes a profession but gives it all up, he will never be saved, because he was never born again to begin with, he was never truly changed by grace divine. On the other hand, the reason he endures to the end is not because of any particular perseverance of his own. What I believe in, and what the Word of God clearly teaches, is the perseverance of the Holy Spirit. When He begins a work, He never gives up until it is completed. That is our confidence.

EXPERIENCE AND FAITH

Forty-three years ago the Spirit of God in grace led me to trust the Lord Jesus Christ. I have had many up-and-downs since then, as the old folks used to sing in a camp meeting I attended:

> I am sometimes up and sometimes down,
> But still my soul am heavenly bound.

I have had varied experiences, but the wonderful thing is this, the Holy Spirit of God has never given me up. And if at times I have been wayward and willful and did not immediately bow before God and repent of my waywardness and willfulness, then I found I had to come under the rod, my Father's rod, and He whipped me into subjection until I came to the place where I was ready to confess my failure and be restored to fellowship with Him. But I was just as truly His child while getting a good whipping as I was when the effects of it had restored me to fellowship. Your child does not cease to be your child when you have him over your knee and are using the slipper on him. It is because he is your child and because you want him to grow up to be a well-behaved boy that you do that. And so we believe in the perseverance of the Holy Spirit of God, that having begun the work He will carry it on to completion.

NEW CREATION

In the third place, we base the doctrine of the eternal security of the believer upon the fact of the new creation. In 2 Corinthians 5:17 we read: "Therefore if any man be in Christ, he is a new creature: old things are passed away; behold, all things are become new." That verse may be rendered like this: Therefore if any man be in Christ, this is new creation; old things have passed away, and all things have become new.

What do we mean by new creation? Just this: we were once in the place of death; we were once utterly lost and ruined. How did we get there? Follow me now. It was not by any act of our own. Do you say, "I did not get into the place of spiritual death by any act of my own?" No, you did not. Do you say, "I was not lost because of any act of my own?" No, you were not. But why were you numbered among the lost? Because you were born into the world a member of the old creation of which Adam the first was the head, and every child of Adam's race comes into the world lost and is under sentence of death. And so we read in verse 14, "The love of Christ constraineth us; because we thus judge, that if one died for all, then were all dead."

THE TWO ADAMS

Let me try to make that clear. Here is Adam the first, the head of the old creation, and he was placed on trial in the Garden of Eden. The entire world was represented in him—you were represented in him, I was represented in him. As the Spirit of God says of Levi, "He was yet in the loins of his father, when Melchisedec met him" (Hebrews 7:10), so we, every one of us, were represented there in Adam when the old creation was on trial. Adam failed, and God said, "In the day thou eatest thereof, dying thou shalt die." As a result of that failure the old creation fell down in death, and every person that has ever been born in the world since that time was born down there; no one has been born up here, where Adam the first started, except our Lord Jesus Christ, and His birth was a supernatural one. Therefore, as members of the old creation we were all dead, all lost. But now see what happened—our Lord Jesus Christ came into the world (the written Word here speaks of Him as the living Word) and He stood on this plane of sinlessness. Adam was created sinless but fell; Jesus came, the sinless One, conceived of the Holy Ghost, born of a virgin mother, but He saw men down there in death, and at the cross He went down into death, down to where man was, and came up in grace from death. But He did not come up alone, for God has quickened us together with Christ, so that all who believe in Him are brought up from that place of death; and as at one time we were made partakers of Adam's race, so now we are made partakers of a new creation. What does God do for us now? Does He put us where Adam was before and say, "Now behave yourselves, and you won't die again"? No, He puts us up higher than Adam could ever have gone except by a new and divine creation. "He hath raised us up together, and made us sit together in heavenly places in Christ Jesus" (Ephesians 2:6), and because we belong to this new creation we can never be lost. You were lost because the head of the old creation failed, and you went down with him. You can never be lost unless the head of the new creation falls, and if He does you will go down with Him. But, thank God, He remains on the throne where God Himself has put Him, in token of His perfect satisfaction in the work He accomplished.

You may have heard of the Irishman who was converted but was seized with a dreadful fear that some day he might commit some great sin and lose his soul, that he might be lost after all, and he trembled at the thought. He went to a meeting and heard the words read, "Ye are dead, and your life is hid with Christ in God." "Glory to God!" shouted Pat. "Whoever heard of a man drowning with his head that high above water?" We are linked with Him, we belong to the new creation, and that is why we shall never be lost.

ETERNAL LIFE POSSESSED NOW

In the last place, we rest the truth of the doctrine of the eternal security of the believer upon the fact that the believer is the present possessor of eternal life. It is not merely that if we are faithful to the end we shall receive eternal life. There is a sense in which that is true; there is a sense in which our hope is eternal life. I am a Christian now if I believe on the Lord Jesus Christ; believing on Him I have eternal life, but I have it in a dying body. I am now waiting for the redemption of the body, and when the Lord

Jesus comes the second time He shall change this body of my humiliation and make it like unto the body of His glory. Then I shall have received eternal life in all its fullness, spirit, soul, and body, entirely conformed to Christ. In that sense I am hoping for eternal life. But over and over and over again, Scripture rings the changes on the fact that every believer is at the present time in possession of eternal life. "As Moses lifted up the serpent in the wilderness, even so must the Son of Man be lifted up; that whosoever believeth in Him should not perish, but have eternal life" (John 3:14-15). Adam's life was forfeitable life; he lost his life because of sin. Eternal life is nonforfeitable life, otherwise it would not be eternal. "For God so loved the world, that He gave His only begotten Son, that whosoever believeth in Him should not perish, but have everlasting life" (John 3:16). Everlasting life is life that lasts forever, and we have it now. "He that believeth on the Son hath everlasting life: and he that believeth not the Son shall not see life; but the wrath of God abideth on him" (John 3:36). "Verily, verily, I say unto you, He that heareth My word, and believeth on Him that sent Me, hath everlasting life, and shall not come into condemnation; but is passed from death unto life" (John 5:24).

HIS SHEEP FOLLOW HIM

I have purposely left this point until last because people generally take it for granted it will be the first passage used in taking up this subject. In John 10:27 we are told, "My sheep hear My voice, and I know them, and they follow Me." Notice these three things. It matters not what profession a man makes, if he does not hear the voice of the Son of God he is not a Christian, and therefore the Savior does not know him as His own. No matter what profession he may make, if he does not follow the Lord Jesus Christ, he is only a sham and a fraud and a hypocrite. He may follow for a little while outwardly, like those of whom the apostle Peter speaks, who walk in the way of righteousness and then turn from it. "But it is happened unto them according to the true proverb, The dog is turned to his own vomit again; and the sow that was washed to her wallowing in the mire" (2 Peter 2:22). If that dog had ever been regenerated and become a sheep, if that sow had ever been changed and become a lamb, neither would have gone back to the filth; but, you see, the dog was always a dog, and the sow was always a sow. They were just whitewashed, not washed white, they were never regenerated, and so went back to the old things. But the sheep of Christ are different. "They follow Me," Jesus says. Be careful. Do not profess to be one of His sheep if you do not follow Him. It is the test of reality. There are many people who tell us, "At such and such a time I was converted, I went forward, I signed a card." You can do all of these things and be lost forever. What you need is a new birth; and when you are born again, you get a new life; and when you receive a new life, you love to follow Jesus; and if you do not, you are not a Christian. Think about it; examine your own foundations a bit.

A Dangerous Doctrine?

People say, "If you preach this doctrine of the eternal security of the believer, men will say, 'Well, then it doesn't make any difference what I do, I will get to heaven anyway.'" It makes a tremendous difference what you do. If you do not behave yourself, it shows that you are not a real Christian. I know that a real Christian may fail, but the difference can be seen in Peter and Judas. Peter failed, and failed terribly, but he was genuine, and one look from Jesus sent him out weeping bitterly; his heart was broken to think that he had so dishonored his Lord. But Judas companied with the Lord almost three-and-a-half years and was a devil all the time; he was a thief and was seeking his own interest. He was even made the treasurer of that company and he held the bag, but we read, "He bare [away] what was put therein" (John 12:6), as this has been literally translated. At last remorse overtook him, not genuine repentance, and what was the result? He went and hanged himself. He was never a child of God. There is a great difference, you see, between a Christian and a false professor.

Justified by Faith

"My sheep hear My voice, and I know them, and they follow Me: and I give unto them eternal life." Do you believe it? I do not understand how people can read a passage like that and then talk about a Christian losing his life. It would not be eternal if it could be lost. "And they shall never perish, neither shall any man pluck them out of My hand." The original is very strong here. In the English a double negative makes an affirmative, but in Greek it only strengthens a declaration, "They shall never, no never, perish." It is impossible, it is unthinkable, that one who has eternal life shall ever perish. "My Father, which gave them Me, is greater than all; and no man is able to pluck them out of My Father's hand." Here I am, a poor lost sinner, but the Lord in grace picks me up and saves me, and I am in His hand. And now the Father puts His hand around too, and I am in the hand of the Father and of the Son, and the devil himself cannot get me unless he can loosen those hands. Could you think of any greater security than to be in the hands of the Father and of the Son? "Never perish," "eternal life"—what wondrous words are these! Do not be afraid of God's truth. You might as well be afraid of the beginning of the gospel that God can freely forgive and justify a guilty sinner by faith in the Lord Jesus Christ. People try to put guards around that truth and say, "Yes, you are justified by faith if you have enough good works to add to it." That is not true. It is by faith alone, and good works spring from that. When you know you have eternal life, you will find your heart so filled with love for Christ that you will try to live for His glory.

Objections

There will be certain passages coming up in the minds of different ones, and they will say, "What he has said may sound logical enough, but what about this Scripture and that?" Let me say, there is no possible Scripture that will come to your mind that the present speaker has not considered carefully over and over again. I have not time in one address to go into all these, but I can assure you that having examined them all with the greatest degree of care, I have never been able to find one that can set aside this: "Neither death, nor life, nor angels, nor principalities, nor powers, nor things present, nor things to come, nor height, nor depth, nor any other creature, shall be able to separate us from the love of God, which is in Christ Jesus our Lord." If you have a clear, definite, positive Scripture, do not allow some passage that is perplexing, that is difficult to interpret, that seems somewhat ambiguous, to keep you from believing the positive statement, "He that believeth hath everlasting life." It is because I have a salvation like this to offer to men, it is because God has sent me to proclaim a salvation like this to sinners, that I have confidence in inviting people to come to Jesus, for I know if they get in living touch with my Savior He will make them His forever.

On two Friday evenings the following opportunity was given for objectors to bring in their questions. These are taken up in detail in the pages that follow.

OBJECTIONS ANSWERED

I recently received from a gentleman a tract entitled, "All about the Eternal Security Doctrine." He is afraid that this doctrine may have a tendency to make people careless about their lives. I can sympathize with him in that for this reason: I was a Christian worker in an organization that believed in what is commonly called the Arminian view; that is, when a person gets converted he has a good start for heaven, and then it is up to him to keep on going. As my old instructor used to say, "Getting to heaven is like riding a bicycle: if I stop, I will fall off." I believed that thoroughly, so thoroughly that when people spoke to me about being eternally saved I used to say, "That is a doctrine of the evil one; that would mislead people and lead folks to become careless," until I had a rather rude awakening.

I found our halls were thronged by people who were getting converted over and over again every few weeks. It seemed as though that old hymn, "Ye Must Be Born Again," should really be sung, "Ye must Be Born Again and Again and Again." That puzzled me, for I never read of anything like it in the Bible. Then I found that the falling away doctrine had a tendency to make people very careless indeed. Let me give you a concrete example. A young man in whom I was quite interested had been addicted to a certain sin in his unconverted days. After he professed conversion he turned from that particular sin, but he confessed to me privately that he had gone out in the darkness of the night, when no one knew where he was, and had fallen into the same sin many times. "How can you do it?" I asked him. "Well," he said, "I always make up my mind that I will commit the sin and then get converted again when I come home." I saw from that how dangerous was the doctrine of being saved today and lost tomorrow. The last time

I saw that young man, he said to me, "It's no use; this sin has such a grip on me that I cannot stand it." "Don't yield," I said. "Let me call in several of the others and let us pray with you." So four or five of us knelt and prayed very earnestly, but he rose again and clenched his fists, for he was in great agony, and said, "It's no use. I am going out to sin, but I am coming back to get converted afterwards." I never saw him again, and I do not know what became of him. That, you see, was one effect of this doctrine that a person loses his salvation when he sins but can come back again and get converted any time he desires. Certainly the Word of God teaches nothing like that. You can see that the Arminian view can be used to turn the grace of God into lasciviousness. It is possible for the other view to be misused also. But I want you to see that the misuse of any doctrine does not in itself prove the teaching is wrong. We need definite Scripture upon which to base our faith. If people have no conscience toward God, they can misuse any doctrine in the Bible. But what we want to get at is this: Are the objections brought against the doctrine of eternal security really tenable?

Question 1. "Is not man an absolutely free moral agent?" as one objector insists. He says, "We can quote no Scripture on unconditional eternal security, because there is none."

I do not know what he means, but of course there is no eternal security that is not based on personal faith in the Lord Jesus Christ. But this writer goes on to say, "When a man is saved, he is on God's altar to live or die, for service or sacrifice, and neither the devil nor demons can pull him off so long as he chooses by God's grace to keep himself in that place."

The fact of the matter is that man is not an "absolutely free moral agent." In his unsaved state he is the slave of sin "led by the devil captive at his will." When regenerated he is the servant of Christ, delighting in holiness and indwelt by the Spirit of the living God. I was not saved by placing my all on the altar. I was saved when I trusted Christ who gave Himself as the offering for my sin. I am not keeping saved by my surrendered life. I am "kept by the power of God." The same grace that saved is the grace that keeps.

I do not simply "choose" to keep myself in the place where I am secure. God has chosen me, and I say amen to His choice. But if it were possible for me to choose to abandon Christ, would I not perish? Yet the Word tells me that Christ's sheep shall never perish. Let us look again at the words of the Lord Jesus in John 10:27-29: "My sheep hear My voice, and I know them, and they follow Me: and I give unto them eternal life; and they shall never perish, neither shall any man pluck them out of My hand. My Father, which gave them Me, is greater than all; and no man is able to pluck them out of My Father's hand."

I wish you would look at verse 27. Who is a sheep of Christ? He is one who hears His voice and follows Him. If a man says, "I am a Christian," but does not hear the voice of the Good Shepherd and does not follow Him, that man is a hypocrite; he is not a Christian. Jesus says, "My sheep hear My voice, and I know them, and they follow Me." Notice the expression, "I know them." I pointed out in my former address that in Matthew 7:22-23, the Lord Jesus says, "Many will say to Me in that day, Lord, Lord, have we not prophesied in Thy name? and in Thy name have cast out devils? and in Thy name done many wonderful works? And then will I profess unto them, I never knew you: depart from Me, ye that work iniquity." Observe that according to Scripture He never says to any soul in the day of judgment, "I used to know you, but I do not know you now." He says, "I *never* knew you." That ought to clear up the whole question. He says of His sheep, "My sheep hear My voice, and I know them." Therefore, if one has ever been a sheep of Christ, the Lord Jesus knows him. Now if by some strange metamorphosis that sheep of Christ were changed into a goat, one of the devil's goats, and appeared at the day of judgment among the goats, Jesus could not say to that goat, "I never knew you." He would have to say, "I used to know you but I do not know you now." But He says, "I *never* knew you," because He gives His sheep eternal life. What is eternal life? One asks, "If the spiritual life of Adam were conditional, how could the life of a believer be secure? Adam must have been eternal in nature." This shows how little well-meaning people distinguish between the life that God gave to Adam by creation and the life that He gives to us by regeneration. Adam's life was simply natural life and he forfeited that when he sinned, but God gives to believers eternal life, and that can never be forfeited. It would not be eternal life if it could. So He says, "I give unto them eternal life, and they shall never perish." He puts no conditions around that promise, "They shall never perish." The word "perish" is in the middle voice, so that if rendered literally in English, you would have to make two words of it, because we do not have a middle voice. The words "perish" and "destroy" are the same in Greek. "I give unto them eternal life, and they shall never destroy themselves."

Sheep so easily destroy themselves. I was going over the desert when out among the Indians, and as we passed a bridge over a deep chasm, we heard the pitiable bleating of a lamb. We went to the edge of the bridge and saw the lamb about fifty feet down on a little ledge. It was a sheer descent of nearly two hundred feet to the creek below that. We looked to see whether there was any possible way to get down there, and we could not find any. That lamb had been eating and had come to the edge and had looked down. There was that little ledge all green, and so down he went and ate all the green that was there before he found that he could not get back. We tried to lasso him, but were not expert enough to do that. We looked up, and already there were three great buzzards flying around, just waiting for the time when the little animal would give up. That lamb was destroying himself. Jesus says, "My sheep will never destroy themselves. I give unto them eternal life and they shall never perish" (in the middle voice, "never perish themselves"). Why not? Because they have the Holy Spirit dwelling in them.

The Word of God says, "Being confident of this very thing, that He who hath begun a good work in you will perform it until the day of Jesus Christ." Jesus first says, "I give unto them eternal life," and then, "They shall never perish, neither shall any man pluck them out of My hand."

Eternal Security 25

Some may say, "Well, I know a devil cannot pluck me out, no angel would want to, and man could not, but I might pluck myself out." Then you would perish, would you not? And He says "They shall never perish," before He tells you, "neither shall any pluck them out of My hand." Is man an absolutely free moral agent? He was when God created him, but is he now? Is the sinner a free moral agent? What does Scripture say? "Ye are led by the devil captive at his will." What? A man led by the devil captive at his will is a free agent? "Know ye not, that he to whom ye yield yourselves servants to obey, his slaves ye are?" (Romans 6:16). Man is a slave to sin and Satan; he is not free. But now the gospel comes to the man, and he does have the power of decision, and when he decides for Christ he gets eternal life with all that that implies, and that life is the same life that is in the blessed Son of God. It is communicated to him, and now he is led captive in the chains of love to the Savior's feet, and he does not want to be a free agent. He is glad to be a bondman, as Paul puts it, of Jesus Christ.

Question 2. What about Matthew 24:13? "But he that shall endure unto the end, the same shall be saved." Weymouth says, "He who stands firm unto the end."

The writer of this question recognizes that primarily this refers to the great tribulation, but it is a principle that I believe every preacher of the Word should insist on. There is no use in people professing conversion, going forward, raising their hands, going to an inquiry room, joining the church, getting baptized, taking communion, teaching a Sunday school class, doing missionary work, giving their money for Christ's work, and going on like this for years, and then by-and-by drifting away, turning from it all, denying the Lord that bought them, refusing absolutely the authority of Jesus Christ, and yet professing to be saved. It is endurance that proves the reality of a work of grace within the soul. That is the difference between one who is merely reformed by the teaching of Christianity and one who has been born again. You see this very clearly when you contrast Peter and Judas.

Peter slipped and sinned grievously, but in spite of it all he endured to the end. Jesus said, "I have prayed for thee that thy faith fail not," and though his outward life for a brief period was not what it should be, his faith remained, and Jesus restored him, and he went on to the end of his life until crucified for his Savior. Judas was one of the chosen, he was with the apostolic band but never was regenerated, and so when he sinned and sold his Lord, he turned away an apostate and died a suicidal death. Jesus said of him long before, "Have not I chosen you twelve, and one of you *is* a devil?" Not, "One of you is in danger of becoming a devil," but "One of you is a devil." And we are told: "Judas by transgression fell, that he might go to his own place" (Acts 1:25). Peter was a backslider, Judas was an apostate, and there is a great difference between the two. If a man says, "I am saved," let him prove it by going on. That is why I say we should not be afraid of the doctrine of the eternal security of the believer. Some say, "But I knew a man who was a wonderful Christian, and now he has given it all up and says he is still saved." He is only deceiving himself. The next time you see him you tell him that the Bible says, "He that shall endure unto the end, the same shall be saved." There is no use your carrying on a profession if your life does not prove it to be real. Men can misuse any doctrine.

Question 3. What about the Scripture found in John 8:31? "Then said Jesus to those Jews which believed on Him, If ye continue in My word, then are ye My disciples indeed." Is not the condition for permanent discipleship "if ye continue in My word?"

Certainly. Every man who knows the truth of eternal security believes it. There is no use for a person to profess to be a disciple of Jesus if he does not continue. It is this that proves there is a genuine work of the Spirit of God in his soul.

Question 4. What about John 6:66? "From that time many of His disciples went back, and walked no more with Him."

That has happened down through the centuries. Jesus distinguishes between a disciple and "a disciple indeed," or between one who is only a disciple and one who is a true believer. The Greek word translated "disciple" means "a pupil" or "a learner." There were many who up to a certain point learned of Jesus, and they were learning more and more every day as they listened to Him. But when He declared, "Whoso eateth My flesh, and drinketh My blood, hath eternal life" (John 6:54), they said, "That is too much for us; we are not going on with this man," and they went back. It was not a question there of whether people were born again and lost, but whether they who had been numbered among the learners would go on learning and let Him be their teacher, or whether they would refuse further instruction and turn back. We are not told that even those who turned back ever again returned.

Question 5. John 6:67, "Will ye also go away?" What about this question?

The question and the answer bring out the very thing I am speaking of. He turned now to the apostles, that little group who had accompanied Him so long, and said, "Will ye also go away?" and Peter said what every truly converted soul always says, "Lord, to whom shall we go? Thou hast the words of eternal life" (John 6:68). If you are really born again, that is always the answer. I remember reasoning on this subject with a dear good brother for something like two hours one day, and he was insisting that a man could take himself out of the Lord's hand. I said, "Why do you keep insisting on this? Are you sure that you are saved?" He said, "Absolutely." "How long?" I asked him. "Forty years," he replied. "And you have been kept for forty years? Do you want to take yourself out of the Lord's hand that you are talking like that?" "Certainly not," he answered. "Well," I said, "you are better than your creed."

That is just the point. If a man is born again, he never wants to take himself out of Christ's hand even if he could. Christ alone is the one who satisfies the soul.

Question 6. How about 2 Thessalonians 2:3? "Let no man deceive you by any means: for that day shall not come, except there come a falling away first, and that man of sin be revealed, the son of perdition."

The word translated "falling away" is "apostasy" in the original. That has nothing to do with the question of individual salvation. It does not touch this doctrine. Can you not see that it is a prophecy of what is happening all about us at the present time? Recently, we were told that seventy-five per cent of the ministers in the church federation in the city of Chicago signed a questionnaire saying that they did not believe in some of the great fundamental truths of the Bible. There you have apostasy. Does that mean that these ministers were all Christians once and now are not saved? My dear friends, I am afraid the whole trouble is that most of them have never been born again at all. They do not know anything of regenerating grace and therefore are quite ready to apostatize from the doctrines held sacred by the great evangelical denominations. I remember when a certain preacher came out with a blatant attack on the doctrine of blood atonement. It shocked a lot of people who had been reading his books, and they said, "Isn't it strange that a man who was once such a fine Christian now denies the blood of Christ?" I sat down and read every one of his books and found that he never mentioned in any of them the blood of Christ or Christ's death on the cross, except in one when he spoke of the example of humiliation Jesus set by going to the cross. But there was never one other reference to the death, the blood, or the atonement. Later he stated: "They charge me with giving up the doctrine of blood atonement; I never believed it." He showed that he was simply an apostate. These things had no place in his heart or life. The apostasy is coming; it is coming fast. The great professing church is going into it, but not one born again person will ever bow to the Antichrist.

Question 7. What about Hebrews 12:14? "Follow peace with all men, and holiness, without which no man shall see the Lord."

That is exactly what we stand for. Anyone who says "I am a Christian" and does not follow peace and holiness will never see the Lord. But I remember how that used to trouble me. When a young Christian, I was taught that when I was converted all my sins up to that moment were put away, and then it was as though God said, "I have wiped off the past and have put you back where Adam was before he fell: if you can keep the record clear from now to the end, you will be saved and you will get to heaven." I started out and soon began to fail, and then they said to me, "The trouble with you is you have not gotten holiness yet. If you get that you will be able to live the right kind of a life." I asked, "What is this blessing of holiness?" and was told, "When God saved you, He only justified you." *Only* justified you? "He forgave your past sin, but now you have to get sanctified, and that means you must have all your inbred sin rooted out, and you will get true holiness." I thought, "But it didn't work very well with Adam," and it rather bothered me. Yet they assured me that was the thing, and so I went in for it and for six years I struggled. (For a more thorough treatment of this subject, see *Holiness: The False and the True*, Loizeaux Brothers.)

I was working on a text that is not in the Bible: "Without holiness no man shall see the Lord." I heard many sermons preached on it, and sometimes I preached on it myself. I had a large red banner with that text in white letters, and I tried to get holiness. Sometimes I thought I had it, and then something would go wrong and I would have to try to get it all over again. I shall never forget the first time I read, "Follow peace with all men, and holiness, without which no man shall see the Lord." I thought it said, "Without holiness it is impossible to see God." I thought I had to get perfect holiness in this life, but what it says there is, if you do not follow holiness you will not see the Lord. Every Christian follows holiness. A man who says "I am a Christian" and does not follow holiness is either self-deceived or a hypocrite. I maintain this with all my heart.

Question 8. What about Romans 6:16? "Know ye not, that to whom ye yield yourselves servants to obey, his servants ye are to whom ye obey; whether of sin unto death, or of obedience unto righteousness?"

I have already spoken of that. Romans 6 is like the book of Exodus. When the children of Israel were in Egypt they obeyed Pharaoh because they had to; when they were brought to God in the wilderness, Pharaoh's power was broken and they became the servants of God. We, in our unsaved days, were servants to sin; now, as Christians, we are servants of God and we are to walk before God in holiness and righteousness.

Question 9. Ezekiel 18:24: "But when the righteous turneth away from his righteousness, and committeth iniquity, and doth according to all the abominations that the wicked man doeth, shall he live?"

Is it not strange for anyone in this dispensation of grace to quote a passage like that, as though it had anything to do with the question of the soul's salvation? Go back and read Ezekiel 18. Of what is it treating? We read in verse 21: "If the wicked will turn from all his sins that he hath committed, and keep all My statutes, and do that which is lawful and right, he shall surely live, he shall not die." Is that grace? No, that is law. That is just the quintessence of law. Do you believe that if a wicked man turns from his wickedness he will live? If this is true, why did Jesus die? Would you preach that to sinners? Would you have me stand up and say, "You wicked people, you have been doing wickedness; you start in tonight to do righteousness and you will live"? Would you have me preach that? I would be deliberately deceiving people if I told them that. But you see, here God was testing people under law and said, "The man that doeth these things shall live. . . . But when the righteous turneth away from his righteousness, and committeth iniquity, and doeth according to all the abominations that the wicked man doeth, shall he live? All his righteousness that he hath done shall not be mentioned in his trespass that he hath trespassed, and in his sin that he hath sinned, in them shall he die." And what has happened? Not one man ever continued in all the things that

Eternal Security 31

are written in the book of the law to do them. Therefore, they were all under sentence of death. How then were they to be saved? By turning over a new leaf? Oh, no—but by confessing that they had no righteousness. If they had, it would only be filthy rags. But now they find all their righteousness in the Lord Jesus Christ, "who of God is made unto us wisdom, righteousness, sanctification, and redemption." Do not ever quote Ezekiel 18 as though it were gospel; it is law. And remember the "life" spoken of in Ezekiel is not eternal life in Christ. It is life here on earth prolonged under the divine government, because of obedience, or cut short because of sin.

Question 10. What about 2 Peter 2:20-22? "For if after they have escaped the pollutions of the world through the knowledge of the Lord and Savior Jesus Christ, they are again entangled therein, and overcome, the latter end is worse with them than the beginning. For it had been better for them not to have known the way of righteousness, than, after they have known it, to turn from the holy commandment delivered unto them. But it is happened unto them according to the true proverb, The dog is turned to his own vomit again; and the sow that was washed to her wallowing in the mire."

Does it say, "But it is happened unto them according to the true proverb, The sheep is turned to its own vomit again"? No, it does not. It says, "The dog is turned to his own vomit again." How many of these dogs there are! They escape the pollution of the world temporarily by the knowledge that comes through the Lord Jesus Christ. If you were brought up in a Christian home and taught the knowledge of the Lord Jesus Christ from your youth, you escaped a great deal of the pollution of the world. But after you have known all these things, you can turn aside; you can take your own way into the world and live in its filth and pollutions. What does that prove? That you used to be a Christian and are not now? That you used to be one of Christ's sheep but are no longer? Oh, no. What then? It proves that "the dog has gone back to his own vomit again, and the sow that was washed to her wallowing in the mire." The remarkable thing about this doctrine of the eternal security of the believer is that many of the greatest men of God who have ever lived have believed in it. C. H. Spurgeon, D. L. Moody, Dr. R. A. Torrey, Dr. A. C. Dixon, and scores of others whom we revere believed in it. C. H. Spurgeon said very beautifully, "If this dog had ever been born again and gotten a sheep's nature, it never would have gone back to its own vomit; and if this sow had ever been regenerated and had the heart of a lamb put in it, it never would have gone back to its wallowing in the mire." It is not a question of a sheep of Christ perishing. The devil has a lot of washed sows, but they are not, and never have been, Christ's sheep.

Question 11. Now we come to the crucial text, Hebrews 6:4-6.

Watch this carefully. See if I read it correctly. "For it is *quite* possible for those who were once enlightened, and have tasted of the heavenly gift, and were made partakers of the Holy Ghost, and have tasted the good word of God, and the powers of the world to come, if they shall fall away, to *renew them again* unto repentance; seeing they crucify to themselves the Son of God afresh, and put Him to an open shame." Is that what it says? You believe that a man can be once enlightened, made a partaker of the Holy Ghost, can taste the good Word of God and the powers of the world to come, but fall away and then repent—don't you? That is what all the folk believe who do not believe in the eternal security of the believer. What are you going to do with your backslider? If backsliding and apostasy are the same, don't you see this passage is the worst possible passage in all the Bible for their favorite doctrine?

If those who hold that a man can be saved over and over again will ponder this passage, I am sure they will see how fatally it knifes their theory.

This is the way it reads: "For it is *impossible* for those who were once enlightened, and have tasted of the heavenly gift, and were made partakers of the Holy Ghost, and

Eternal Security

have tasted of the good Word of God, and the powers of the world to come, if they shall fall away to renew them again unto repentance; seeing they crucify to themselves the Son of God afresh, and put Him to an open shame." If this passage teaches that a man once saved can be lost again, then it also teaches that if that man is lost again, he can never repent and be saved. In other words, if that passage teaches that a man once saved can be lost again, it teaches that if you have ever been saved and you are now lost, you have a one-way ticket for hell, and there is no turning back. But what is the real question here? It is almost impossible to explain it in a minute or two, for you need to study the entire fifth and sixth chapters of Hebrews together.

The apostle is speaking to people who have the Old Testament and have been intellectually convinced that Jesus is the Messiah but who are exposed to persecution if they confess His name. Even if not genuine, they know that Jesus is the Messiah, and they must have felt the power and seen the evidence of His authority in the miracles wrought. Yet they can turn their backs upon it all and go back to Judaism, and go into the synagogue again and say, "We do not believe Jesus Christ is the Messiah, the Son of God; we refuse the authority of this man. He should be crucified." "They crucify to themselves the Son of God afresh, and put Him to an open shame." The apostle says, "Do not try to do anything there; you cannot, for they have gone too far. They are apostate." It proves that they are not real Christians. In verse 9 we read, "But, beloved, we are persuaded better things of you, and things that accompany salvation, though we thus speak." That is, you could have all these things and not have salvation. You say, "I don't think so." But look at it: "It is impossible for those who were once enlightened." What does that mean? Born again? No one could listen to a gospel address without being enlightened. "The entrance of Thy words giveth light, it giveth understanding unto the simple" (Psalm 119:130).

". . . and have tasted of the heavenly gift." It is one thing to taste; it is another thing to eat. Many a person has gone that far and never been saved. The angel said to Ezekiel, "Son of man, eat this roll." But the angel saw that Ezekiel had only tasted it, so he commanded, "Son of man, cause thy belly to eat it." It was in his mouth, and if his head had been cut off all the truth would be gone, but "God desires truth in the inward parts."

". . . and were made partakers of the Holy Ghost." They were neither sealed, nor indwelt, nor baptized, nor filled with the Spirit. He does not use one of the terms that refer to the Spirit's great offices, but says, "and were made partakers of the Holy Ghost." Did you ever see a man in a meeting where the Spirit of God was working in power, and have you ever gone over and talked to him and said, "Don't you want to come to Christ?" And he has answered, "I know I ought to come, I can feel the power of the Spirit of God in this meeting. I know this thing is right and I ought to yield, but I don't want to, and I won't." And he goes away resisting the Spirit although he was a partaker. So these people described in Hebrews 6 had been in this way outwardly acquainted with Christianity, but they now denied it all. For such there could be no repentance.

Now in order to prove that this is the correct interpretation of the passage, let me draw your attention to Hebrews 6:7-9: "For the earth which drinketh in the rain that cometh oft upon it, and bringeth forth herbs meet for them by whom it is dressed, receiveth blessing from God: but that which beareth thorns and briers is rejected, and is nigh unto cursing; whose end is to be burned. But, beloved, we are persuaded better things of you, and things that accompany salvation, though we thus speak." Notice in the first place, all these things he speaks of in verses 4-5 might be true of a man and yet he would not have salvation. But he says, as it were, "Though we have given you this warning, we are persuaded better things of you; you have gone farther than these apostates ever did, you have been saved; and so do not think we are confounding you with people like these." He uses this little parable to make clear what he means. Here are two pieces of grass growing side by side, we will say, just separated by a fence. The earth is the same, the same sun shines on them both, the same kind of rainfall waters them both. When the time of harvest comes, one of these plots brings forth herbs, but the other only thorns and briers. What is he teaching here? This is a message to the Jews, trying to make them see the reality of Christ's messiahship and His fulfillment of all the types of old. These two plots of ground are two men, they are the hearts of two men. We may think of them in this way to make it all more graphic. They grow up side by side; they both are taught the Bible; they both go to the same synagogue; both wait for the Messiah; both go down and listen to John the Baptist preach; perhaps both were baptized by John the Baptist, confessing their sins. John's baptism was not salvation; it was just looking forward to the coming of a Savior. Both of them hear the Lord Jesus; both of them see Him do His works of power; both are in that crowd watching when He dies; both are there when the throngs go out to see the open tomb; both are near when He ascends to heaven; both see the mighty work of the Spirit on the day of Pentecost; both of them move in and out among the apostles; and outwardly you could not see any difference between them. But by-and-by persecution breaks out. One of them is arrested, and they say to him, "Deny Jesus Christ, or you will die." He says, "I cannot deny Him; He is my Savior." "Then you will die," the first one declares. "I am ready to die, but I cannot deny Him," the second man replies. The other one is arrested and they say, "You must deny Christ or die." He says, "I will deny Him rather than die. I will go back and be a good Jew again rather than die." "Come out here, then," they command him.

They had a terrible way of taking him back. I remember reading how in such a case, they took him to an unclean place where a man slew a sow, and this one going back to Judaism, in order to prove his denial, spits on the blood of the sow and says, "So count I the blood of Jesus the Nazarene." And then they purify him and take him back. Could any real believer in Jesus do that? What made the difference between the two?

Those plots of ground had the same rain, the same sunshine, but there were different crops. What was the difference? One of them had the good seed and brought forth good fruit; the other did not have the good seed and brought forth thorns and briers. These two men were both familiar with the truth, but one received the incorruptible seed, the Word of life, and brought forth fruit unto God. The other has never received the good seed, and the day comes when he is an apostate.

If you will keep in mind the difference between an apostate and a backslider, it will save you a lot of trouble over many Scriptures. The apostate knows all about Christianity but never has been a real Christian. The backslider is a person who has known Christ, who did love Him, but became cold in his soul, lost out in his spiritual life. There is not a Christian who has not often been guilty of backsliding. That is why we need the Lord as our advocate to restore our souls. When backslidden, it is not our *union* with Him that is destroyed, but it is our *communion*. You may say, "Why are you so sure that a real Christian does not apostatize?" Because God says so in His Word. 1 John 2:18: "Little children, it is the last time: and as ye have heard that antichrist shall come, even now are there many antichrists; whereby we know that it is the last time." Antichrist means "opposed to Christ." The apostate is always a man opposed to Christ. A man says, "I have tried it all, and there is nothing in it," and so denounces Christ. "They went out from us, but they were not of us; for if they had been of us, they would no doubt have continued with us: but they went out, that they might be made manifest that they were not all of us." The words "no doubt" are in italics and really cast a doubt. Leave those words out for they do not belong in the Greek text, and read it, "They went out from us, but they were not of us: for if they had been of us, they would have continued with us." And then he adds, "They went out, that they might be made manifest that they were not altogether (that is the literal rendering) of us" (1 John 2:19). In other words, they were with us in profession, in outward fellowship, but not altogether of us, because they had never really been born of God. This also explains Hebrews 10 which is the next passage brought up here as an objection.

Question 12. Explain Hebrews 10:28-29: "He that despised

Moses' law died without mercy under two or three witnesses: of how much sorer punishment, suppose ye, shall he be thought worthy, who hath trodden under foot the Son of God, and hath counted the blood of the covenant, wherewith he was sanctified, an unholy thing, and hath done despite unto the Spirit of grace?" People are troubled here, for they say, "Well, this man was surely a Christian, because it says that he was sanctified."

That does not necessarily prove that he was a Christian. The whole nation of Israel was sanctified by the blood of the covenant; in a certain sense the whole world has been sanctified by the blood of the cross. If it were not for that blood shed on Calvary's cross the whole world would be doomed to eternal judgment, but because Jesus died for the entire world God says, "Now, I can deal with all men on the ground of the blood of the cross," and, as we often put it, the great question between God and man today is not primarily the sin question. Why? Because the blood of Christ answers for sin. What is the great question? It is the Son question: How are you treating God's Son who died to save you? Christ has died for all men, His blood is shed for the salvation of all men, and it will avail for every sinner in all the world if they trust Him. (See John 3:18-19.)

Here is this Hebrew who has followed along to a certain point, and now the question comes, "Will you confess this Christ as your one great sin offering no matter what it means?" And he answers, "No, I cannot do that. I am going back to the temple. There is a sin offering there, and I will not have to suffer as I may if I confess Jesus Christ." But he cannot do that. God does not accept any more that "there remaineth no more sacrifice for sins." "If we sin willfilly after that we have received the knowledge of the truth, there remaineth no more sacrifice for sins." "There remaineth no *other* sacrifice for sins" is the true meaning. This sacrifice at the altar was commanded by God. He said, "If you sin, you must bring a sacrifice, and I will accept you." "The life of the flesh is in the blood: and I have given it to you upon the altar to make an atonement for your souls: for it is the blood that maketh an atonement for the soul" (Leviticus 17:11). "All right," this Jew says, "I have a sin offering." But he has met Jesus Christ or heard of Him as the great sin offering; he knows that God accepted Him and raise Him from the dead; he has all this knowledge, but having it all he is afraid to come out definitely and confess Christ as his Savior. He says, "I do not need this sin offering; I will go back and be content with the sin offering of the temple." Before Jesus came, that was acceptable because it pointed to Him, but now He has come. If you reject Him, there remains no other offering. This passage, you see, has nothing to do with a real Christian turning from Christ, but with a man thoroughly instructed who refuses to accept Him. And how many people there are, not only among the Jews but in Christendom, who are refusing this sin offering.

Question 13. The next passage brought up is Luke 9:61-62: "And another also said, Lord, I will follow Thee; but let me first go bid them farewell, which are at home at my house. And Jesus said unto him, No man, having put his hand to the plough, and looking back, is fit for the kingdom of God."

What a terrible thing it would be if this were the way into heaven! How many thousands of earnest Christian people there are who have allowed what they thought was their responsibility to their friends to keep them from fully following Christ. Suppose they went to heaven only on the ground of fully following Him. You see, these Jews were looking for the kingdom, and many said, "I will follow Thee, but my friends have a claim on me." "No," the Lord says, "I must come first. No man, having put his hand to the plough, and looking back, is fit for the kingdom of God." That is the test of discipleship. But it is necessary to distinguish between salvation by grace and reward for faithful discipleship. The rewards are connected with the kingdom. No matter how faithful I may be as a Christian, it does not give me any better place in heaven than if I were taken there the moment I was saved. Suppose the very instant you were converted you dropped dead—would you have gone to heaven? Yes, you would have gone there on the ground of God's delight in the work of His Son. Suppose you were converted fifty years ago. There have been ups-and-downs in your life, but you have been saved all those years. Where would you go if you died suddenly? You would go to heaven. On what ground? On the ground of God's delight in the work of His Son. There is not a bit of change in fifty years. "But," you say, "I have been a wonderfully faithful Christian." Have you, indeed? I am surprised that you should think so. The more we serve Him, the more most of us feel how unfaithful we have been. But you insist, "I have been a very faithful Christian." Does that make you any more fit for heaven than you were the moment you trusted Jesus? You ask, "Does faithfulness as a disciple go for nothing?" It goes for a great deal, but it has no saving merit. You have a place in the Father's house on the ground of pure grace, but the Father's house is not the only thing before us. There is also the kingdom of God. "Then shall the righteous shine forth in the kingdom of their Father." And here there are different rewards according to the measure of faithfulness in this life.

Here was one to whom the Lord said, "I want you to follow Me to Africa or India," and he said, "O Lord, suffer me first to go and bury my father. I have an old father here and cannot bear to leave him as long as he lives. After he is dead, I am willing to follow Thee." And the Lord says, "Let the dead bury their dead." Of course, if he had the responsibility of providing for his father, that would be a different thing. Because that man has not the faith and courage to make that break, does he cease to be a Christian? He may stay at home, he may be of great value and great use, but when he comes to the judgment seat of Christ there is a reward he might have had that he will not have, because he did not go the whole way with the Lord Jesus Christ. If going the whole way entitled men to heaven, none of us would ever get there. But as we go the whole way, as far as we understand, He is going to reward us. If people could learn to see the difference between salvation by grace and reward for service, this question would settle itself. From this point on, most of these objections really have to do with this very fact.

Question 14. Take the next one, Hebrews 3:12-14: "Take heed, brethren, lest there be in any of you an evil heart of unbelief, in departing from the living God. But exhort one another daily, while it is called Today; lest any of you be hardened through the deceitfulness of sin. For we are made partakers of Christ, if we hold the beginning of our confidence stedfast unto the end." That is one of the "if" verses. Another one is found in 1 Corinthians 15:1-2: "Moreover, brethren, I declare unto you the gospel which I preached unto you, which also ye have received, and wherein ye stand; by which also ye are saved, if ye keep in memory what I preached unto you, unless ye have believed in vain." Another one is found in Colossians 1:21-23: "And you, that were sometime alienated and enemies in your mind by wicked works, yet now hath He reconciled in the body of His flesh through death, to present you holy and unblameable and unreproveable in His sight: if ye continue in the faith grounded and settled, and be not moved away from the hope of the gospel, which ye have heard, and which was preached to every creature which is under heaven; whereof I Paul am made a minister." I might add others to these, but here are three "ifs."

What does the Spirit of God mean by bringing these "ifs" in? In every one of these instances He is addressing bodies of people. I stand here to address you as a body of people. If I were to ask everybody who professes to be a Christian to stand, I suppose nearly everybody would rise. Would that prove that you are all Christians? It would show that you *profess to be* Christians. What would prove that you really are? "If ye continue in the faith grounded and settled, and be not moved away from the hope of the gospel." You profess to have received the gospel; you are saved if you keep in memory what has been preached unto you. If you do not, it just shows that there is no reality.

The faith here is not the faith by which you are saved, it is not the faith by which you believe; but it is that which you believe. Jude says, "Earnestly contend for the faith which was once delivered unto the saints" (Jude verse 3). That is the body of Christian doctrine, and, if a real Christian, you will stand for that Christian doctrine to the end; but if not, you may become a Mormon, or a Christian Scientist, or a theosophist, or something like that. Then you simply show there is no reality. It is a very easy thing to say, "I am saved"; it is another thing to prove it.

Question 15. What of 2 Peter 3:17? "Ye therefore, beloved, seeing ye how these things before, beware lest ye also, being led away with the error of the wicked, fall from your own stedfastness."

We come back to what we were speaking of a few minutes ago. There is always a possibility of a real Christian falling, and we need to be warned again and again. How many we have known who at one time had a bright Christian testimony but fell? They were not watchful, they were not prayerful, and they stumbled and fell. Does that mean they are lost? No, not if really born again. If born again, they have received eternal life; and if people thus fall, that is where the restoring work of the Spirit of God comes in. David fell in a most terrible way, but he says, "He restoreth my soul"; and sometimes in restoring His people's souls, God has to put them through very bitter experiences. He loves them too much to let them be happy when away from Him.

Question 16. Explain this passage "Who concerning the truth have erred, saying that the resurrection is past already; and overthrow the faith of some" (2 Timothy 2:18). A writer says, "We see here the possibility of having our faith overthrown."

That's not what Paul is talking about. He is speaking of *the* faith. Again you must make the distinction. Our faith is that by which we believe. We believe God; that is faith. But we believe the truth that God has revealed to us, and that truth is *the* faith, and that is what has been overthrown in the mind of the professed believer in this instance. That is the same thing that you get in 1 Timothy 5:15: "For some are already turned aside after Satan." Some real Christians do that, but what a blessed thing to know the Lord goes after them and never gives them up.

Question 17. May we not let the things of God slip away from us? "Therefore we ought to give the more earnest heed to the things which we have heard, lest at any time we should let them slip" (Hebrews 2:1), or, in other words, "Lest at any time we should drift away from them."

This is the same warning again. You have listened to precious ministry from men of God who have preached the Word to you. You have had such instruction as many never have had. You will be terribly guilty if you drift away from it. You need to "continue in the things which you have learned." But if we were all to lose our salvation every time we drifted into some erroneous thing, how serious it would be! Is there anyone here who has never done a little bit of drifting?

If sin will separate me from Christ, how much sin? How can I ever be sure how much sin? Is there a Christian here who has not sinned today? Is it not a fact that every one of us sins in thought, or word, or in deed, probably every day of our lives? Is there ever a night that you can kneel before God and say, "Lord, I thank You that I have not sinned in thought or word or deed today?" I am sure no honest Christian can say that. How far do you have to sin in order to break the link that binds you to Christ? You never could be sure that you are saved from one day to another and you would not leave any room for the restoring work of God if your salvation depended upon your personal faithfulness.

Question 18. What about such a Scripture as this? "Be thou faithful unto death and I will give thee a crown of life?" *(Revelation 2:10). How can you say that a man is saved for eternity when the Lord says you must be faithful to the end?*

A crown of life is not salvation; it is reward. There are five crowns: the incorruptible crown for faithfully running the course; the crown of rejoicing for winning souls; the crown of righteousness for those who love His appearing; the crown of life for those who suffer for Christ; the crown of glory for those who feed the sheep and lambs of Christ's flock. I might lose all of those crowns and yet not lose my salvation. The Word says, "If any man's work shall be burned. . . . he himself shall be saved; yet so as by fire" (1 Corinthians 3:15). But I do not want to be saved that way. I want to win the crown of life. "Be thou faithful unto death, and I will give thee a crown of life."

Question 19. Explain Hebrews 10:37-39: "For yet a little while, and He that shall come will come, and will not tarry. . . . If any man draw back, My soul shall have no pleasure in him."

Look at the next verse, "But *we* (who? real Christians) are not of them who draw back unto perdition; but of them that believe to the saving of the soul." If a person has believed to the saving of the soul, there is no danger of his "drawing back unto perdition." It is a terrible thing to be intellectually convinced and stop there.

Question 20. Now I am referred to Revelation 3:15-16, where the Lord, speaking to the church at Laodicea, says, "I know thy works, that thou art neither cold nor hot: I would thou wert cold or hot. So then because thou art lukewarm, and neither cold nor hot, I will spue thee out of My mouth."

Is this an individual who has once been saved and is so no longer? The Lord is talking to a church. Did you ever see a church like the one at Laodicea, a church neither hot nor cold, one where you could not tell whether it was for Christ or against Him? And then the Lord says to that church, "Because you are just lukewarm—there is profession—but you are neither hot or cold, I will spit you out of My mouth. I won't own you as a church at all." That does not say that there may not be individuals in the church who are children of God, just as in the church at Ephesus. He said to them, "If you do not repent, I will remove your candlestick." A candle, you know, is to give light.

Every time I go downtown I pass a church that D. L. Moody used to belong to. It was an evangelistic center in the city in his day, but today it is a very center of modernism and the gospel is never preached there. Every time I look at it I think of the time Moody was there and it stood firmly for the truth, and I say, "Their candlestick is removed." There may be some true Christians in that church, some of the dear old people who were in it years ago, and maybe their membership is still there. It does not say that *they* are not Christians because the church as such has lost its witness for Christ.

Question 21. Here is a verse I am surprised to find used to prove the "falling away" doctrine. "If the righteous scarcely be saved, where shall the ungodly and the sinner appear?" (1 Peter 4:18).

What has that to do with the question? What is Peter saying? "The time is come that judgment must begin at the house of God: and if it first begin at us, what shall the end be of them that obey not the gospel of God?" (1 Peter 4:17). I suppose that God's children have faults. I know they have to be judged for their faults by the Father in correction, and God will deal very solemnly and seriously with them about their failures. There would be no need of judgment if they were all perfect Christians, but if God deals with His own people in this way and if the righteous be saved through difficulty, "Where shall the ungodly and the sinner appear?" That has nothing to do with the question of whether the Christian is saved for eternity or not.

Question 22. John 15:1-6 is the next passage questioned.

This chapter is not discussing the question of eternal life but of fruit bearing. There are a great many believers who bear very little fruit for God, but all bear some fruit for Him. There are many people in the vine (and the vine speaks of profession here on earth) who bear no fruit for Him and will eventually be cut out altogether when Jesus comes. There will be no place with Him because there is no union with Him. There are no natural branches in the living vine. We are grafted in by faith. I do not know much about grafting, but I do know that it is one thing to put a graft in, and it is another thing for a graft to strike. It is one thing for a person to be outwardly linked with Him and quite another for that person to have life in Christ. What is the test that proves whether he is really in the vine? The test is if he bears fruit. All who have life bear some fruit for God. If there is no fruit, you can be sure there is no life, no real union with Christ.

Question 23. Will any Christian who passes away with unconfessed sin have an opportunity to make things right after death? Is the judgment seat of Christ the time when all misunderstandings and discords among Christians will be made right?

It is questionable if any Christian ever died who did not have some unconfessed sin to his record. While sin might be confessed in a general way, who of us has ever definitely confessed all his sins? But the precious blood of Christ answers for every sin a believer has ever committed. At the judgment seat of Christ, the Lord will go over the entire life since regeneration, giving His mind about every thing, and the believer will then for the first time see each detail in the light of God's infinite holiness. Everything there will be dealt with so that the believer's failures will never be referred to again for all eternity.

Question 24. Is there any difference between the book of life and the Lamb's book of life?

Yes, the book of life is the book of the living. It is the record too, of profession. From this book names may be blotted out. The Lamb's book of life is the record of the eternal purpose of God. Names inscribed there are written from the foundation of the world. In other words, one book speaks of responsibility, the other of pure grace.

No Christian will ever have his name blotted out of the Lamb's book of life, for all such have eternal life—which is unforfeitable and everlasting.